Life Mastery

QUAZI JOHIR

Copyright © 2018 Quazi Johir

All rights reserved.

ISBN-13: 978-1-9804-5217-1

DEDICATION

This book is dedicated to a cause greater than oneself, the evolution of the collective consciousness. It is my deep wish that you apply one or more, or even none of the principles mentioned in this book to discover your true potential, for when you live your best life, you give the world the best gift; the gift of experiencing your grace.

CONTENTS

	Introduction	i
1	**The Five Principles of Life**	**1**
	Presence	1
	Balance	2
	Love	3
	Impermanence (Unattachment)	4
	Abundance	5
2	**The Fundamental "Currency" of Life: Energy**	**8**
	Low Vibration Energy	8
	High Vibration Energy	9
	Morning Routine to Access HVE	10
	Mid-day Activities	13
	Night-time routine to cleanse energy body	14
	Daily Journaling	15

3	**Manifestation**	**17**
	The All Space	17
	The Power of Thoughts	20
	Desire vs Intent	22
	The 3 Planes of Existence	26
	Self-Image	29
	Letting Go	33
4	**When Things Aren't Going Your Way**	**37**
	Negative Thoughts and their Harmfulness	37
	The 4 Step Process to Eliminate Negative Thoughts	39
	Negativity = Positivity in Disguise	41
	Using Negativity as a Fuel for Presence	43
5	**Life as a Dream**	**46**

INTRODUCTION

Dear reader, thank you for choosing this book, and more importantly, thank you for choosing to take the reins to control your life. Even the word "control" has connotations of resistance and the like, thus from here on "control" will simply be substituted with "choose". This book will outline the principles that will allow you to live a more fulfilling life, and to simply be able to choose the life that you want. You no longer have to battle with the world to get the wealth, the partner of your dreams or even to get that A on your exam. Simply choose it, intend to have it and it is yours. I am very excited to share with you the knowledge that has changed my life and have helped me manifest beautiful things into my own life...things better than I even asked for. Strange, but such is life when you start to love it and realize it is your best friend.

You do not have to take anything in this book as stipulated, all the ideas in this book are a model; in science and in every aspect of life, we tend to develop a model that corresponds with the general idea of things. There is no absolute truth, every model contributes a separate aspect to a reality that is inherently multifaceted. Every model contributes to the grander truth, only we cannot harmonize all these models since our consciousness does not correspond to a high enough level to understand. As you grow in your spiritual journey, and experience life with more breadth, you will start to have new ideas that correspond to your subjective experience of reality. More and more ideas will come, new ideas will come, you will have a shift in paradigms. You will transcend the old model and develop a new one that helps you live better. I hope this book is of use to you. Good luck!

1 THE FIVE PRINCIPLES OF LIFE

Presence

There can never be any problem now, in the present moment, there is no problem. There are problems from the past and in the future, but right now there is none. Think about it. Look at your hands. Realize where you are. Feel the sensations in your limbs, your body. The present moment dissolves all problems.

One of the key principles of life is Presence. When you are in the present moment, you tap into the life energy that rejuvenates you. All inspiration and creativity that was once lost in the turmoil of your thoughts is now returned to you. Essentially, being in the present moment frees up energy tied into "worrying" about the past and the future and lets you channel them into more useful activities that are actually going to help you.

The power of Presence is underestimated. Next time you feel your mind wandering, remember to wake up, for life is nothing more than a dream. If you've ever had lucid dreams, you'll know that you can start controlling them once you "wake up" in the dream itself. So can you imagine what you would be able to do if you could wake up in reality? Most people are so hypnotized by the rules and beliefs ingrained through the norms of social conditioning that it's difficult to wake up. Only a handful of Buddhist monks have been able to tap into that kind of presence energy to wake up in reality.

Aside from 20 minutes of mindful meditation every day, with each passing hour of every day, set an alarm on your phone to remind you to get present. Realize that you're awake and not dreaming. Look at your hands. Look at every single crease in your palm. This practice alone will get you the radiance of present energy. "The Power of Now" by Eckhart Tolle is a good book that teaches you more about Presence.

Balance

Life will always take the path of lowest energy, just as humans will perform the task that requires the least amount of effort. Everything in nature strives to go from a higher potential energy to the lowest potential energy. This is the state of balance.

In everything that you do in life, if you ever find yourself asking "is this too much?" you will know that you've reached the point where more will disturb the balance. When you disturb the balance of life, life will act to restore the balance.

An example of this can be understood by the laws of gravity. When you stand on the flat surface of the earth, at the lowest point, the energy potential is zero, which is where nature wants you. However, when you stand on top of a ledge on the highest cliff, you develop a fear; one wrong step and life will end. This fear generates a higher energy potential, and nature acts to balance this potential by making you take a wrong step and throwing you down the cliff, or merely making you step off the ledge and returning you to a flat surface. This idea is further illustrated in "Transurfing Reality" by Vadim Zeland, but for the purposes of this book (and life), all you need to know is that Balance is a fundamental principle of life towards which everything strives, whether it be emotions, habits, actions...everything.

Love

Most ideas of love are misconstrued. There is unconditional love and conditional love. Independent love and dependent love is a better way of describing it.

I'll begin by describing the latter first.

Conditional love is the root of all evil. "I love him because..." or "If she does this, I will do this or love her more..". This dependency creates a reactive frame, because your love for someone else is dependent on conditions. Once you are in a reactive frame, you are no longer in control. Conditional love directly violates the principle of Presence and Balance.
The principle of Presence strives to set you free, and to bask in the Presence energy, but once you get in a reactive frame, you are no longer tapping into Presence.

Conditional love ruins the balance of life through the generation of an energy potential. Once you seek conditions upon which to give someone your love, you are feeding off the energy of the other person's actions, which makes your energy source dependent on external conditions. And any time you rely on an external energy source for your energy, an energy excess is created, which must be balance (a price is paid for relying on external sources of energy). More on this will be described later.

Unconditional love seeks no energy sources. Unconditional love radiates within. Tapping into present energy opens up the door for unconditional love. It is that warm feeling in your solar plexus that radiates outwards. Unconditional loves just because. There is beauty in everything and ugly in everything; finding the beauty will help you more than judging the ugly. Of-course I'm not asking you to be so pompous as to go around spreading your "love for all mankind", but use this law in balance; it is for you to know when any of the principles outlined in this book will help you.

Once you start loving unconditionally, people feel it. You are no longer sucking energy out of people, but energizing them, and being in your presence fulfills them. That's why there are some people who have magnetic personalities; being in their mere presence energizes us. This is especially true of the higher spiritual leaders, in the presence of whom we almost absorb higher knowledge and greater emotions through osmosis.

Impermanence (Unattachment)

Life has ups and downs and behaves like a wave. There will be periods in your life where you experience expansion and periods where you experience contraction. Both are beneficial and both help you grow. It is how you deal with these moments that determines the strength of your character and what you are capable of.

It is key, however, to not get attached to any of these periods. A realization that "This too shall pass" is the attitude that brings about success in any field. The house you're living in, is not forever. The car you're driving, is not forever. The job you're working, not forever. The partner you're with, is not forever. Your family, and even your physical form, not forever. No THING is forever. The sooner you realize that, the closer you get to your higher self. Only Divinity is forever, for it is not a thing and has existed always.

The ever changing nature of life will slowly grow on

you as you age, and with age you will realize that everything is fleeting; humans have an innate fear of change and the unknown, but with time and more experience this fear slowly dissipates and you become more grounded.

Once you start getting attached to something through placing excess importance to it, this will generate an energy potential. Life will then act to reduce this potential energy by taking the thing away from you to restore balance. It's almost like the time when you, as a child, would watch too much TV or play video games and your parents would come in and stop you because they've deemed you've had too much. Again this links to the principle of Balance.

So remember, nothing is forever. Take care to not place too much importance on anything.

Abundance

It's very counterintuitive, but life will reward you with things that you are already abundant in. This is because when you are abundant in something, you radiate the energy that attracts that thing. The more abundant you are in it, the more of it you attract. Ever heard the saying "The rich keep getting richer and the poor keep getting poorer"? This is why. The concept of energy will be discussed later on in the book.

Even though you may not have something now does not mean you will not have it later. We were not put in this world to work 9-5 jobs and slave for a slice of bread. God/Divinity or whatever you want to call this power, did not intend for His/his/Its children to suffer. Would your parents want you to suffer? No, society conditions us to believe that we must do certain things to be deserving of certain rewards. You shape your reality with your beliefs.

For now, it is sufficient to "fake it till you make it"; believe and visualize already having something, being abundant in it, feeling abundant in it, i.e. wealth, partners, love...whatever it is you please. For when you come from a mindset of scarcity, you establish to life that you are not deserving of the things you want, and reality simply reflects your thoughts like a mirror and manifests this scarcity

2 THE FUNDAMENTAL "CURRENCY" OF LIFE: ENERGY

Everything in life can be broken down into energy. All material, thoughts and ideas can be broken down into energy. Everyone radiates a certain energy, which vibrates at a certain frequency. David R. Hawkins, renowned authority in consciousness research, has developed a "Map of Consciousness" which hierarchically places the different levels of consciousness (energy), from 0-1000, and is logarithmic (going from 201-202 is an increase by a power of 10). In this scale, 200 is the neutral point, 1000 is absolute enlightenment and below 200 is life depleting, and above it is life sustaining. For the purposes of our understanding, it is merely sufficient to know that there exists Low Vibration Energy and High Vibration Energy.

Low Vibration Energy

This is the energy that lies below the 200 point on Hawkins' scale. Low Vibration Energy (LVE) aims to suck the life out of you. Here are some characteristics of LVE:

- Manifests as a rushed feeling
- Wants to get somewhere, never present
- Wants to take, not to give
- Wants to fuel conflict, not solve
- Reactive, not proactive
- Hate, not love
- Life depleting not life sustaining (contractive)
- Heavy feeling in the solar plexus area
- Competitive, not collaborative

By the principle of abundance, whatever you are abundant in, you will attract in your life, thus LVE brings more LVE and energy then materializes into events in your life that are Low Vibration, ie accidents and misfortune. If it is one thing that one MUST do, it is to eliminate all LVE from life. But in order to do that, one needs to be energetically aware. More on this later. But right now, it is sufficient to be able to identify LVE through the characteristics given above, no need to try to resist it, but just be able to identify it. Next time you're amongst a group of friends, see how you feel, or how their actions relate to the list, are they contributing to LVE?

collarbone all the way across to the sides, and up and down the sternum. Do this until all surface has been covered. Again, the collarbone also contains important pressure points.

6) <u>Alternating leg tap</u>: Now stand up and use your right hand to tap your (raised) left knee. Alternate for the other set of limbs. Do this for 10 reps then switch the pattern and do it again for 10 reps for a total of 20 reps. This will connect the left and right hemispheres of your brain to begin your day.

7) <u>Alternating breaths</u>: After the leg tap, sit down, rest your left foot on your right knee, place your right hand on your ankle and left hand on top of your right hand such that the fingers go over and extend onto the heel of your left foot. Now sit up straight (relaxed) and take 7 deep breaths in through the nose and out through the mouth. Do this same procedure for the other side (right foot on left knee) and relax. Now, join both of your hands together by the fingertips, like making a crown, and place the thumbs right over the center of your temple (third eye region, or wherever you think your third eye should be). Now repeat the 7 deep breaths. You have now completed joining both brain hemispheres.

8) <u>Energy Flow</u>: Stretch out your spine with your hands extended for 10 seconds. Put your hands down and relax. Now imagine 2 channels extending through your spine to your legs and into the ground and the sky. Take 3 deep breaths in and focus on these energy meridians. Feel energy flowing from the sky to the ground, passing through your body. Feel yourself drawing energy from the heavens and passing it to the Earth. Now take 3 deep breaths from the ground up to the heavens. Inhale from the ground to your center point. Squeeze your kegel (PC muscle) as you inhale and store energy drawn in from the Earth. And on the exhale feel it going from the center point through the top of your head, through your arms, into the heavens. You are now basking in HVE and letting

it flow through you.
9) <u>Ending Energy Scan</u>: Now, do a final energy scan as you did earlier. Do you feel any different? The tingling feeling in your heart area? That is the HVE radiating outwards from your center. Give yourself a final rating out of 10 and you are ready to go.

Note: You don't have to do any of these exercises, or take my word when I say that energetic awareness will change your life. Simply try them for 21 days. Over time, these exercises will take a maximum of 20 minutes out of your morning.

Mid-day activities

As you go about your day, be observant. What kind of energy are you receiving from your environment, from the people? Characterize them according to the list. Try to avoid LVE to the best of your ability, for it will easily latch on to you. Of-course, it isn't always possible to avoid everyone/everything, exercise good judgment.
Reality is like a dream. The key to all spirituality, and tapping into higher levels of consciousness, is to wake up from this dream, such that you can control it. It's like with lucid dreaming, once you realize that it's all a dream, you begin to control it. Imagine what's possible if you can wake up in reality. Throughout the day, practice waking up. Discern whether or not you are dreaming or if this reality is true. Pinch yourself, and look at your hands. Often in dreams, hands get distorted. Practice getting present to the moment every moment. Feel into every step you take and every sensation. I like to do this every hour of the day.

Night-time routine to cleanse energy body

Your day has passed, and it's time for bed. Surely you've accumulated some LVE in your energy body. But you cannot afford a single ounce of LVE in your life, especially the ones stored in your subconscious. The following exercise will help you let go:

LVE Processing Exercise

1) Find something irritating: This could be something that occurred throughout the day, usually something tiny or even large, that led you to feel anxiety or even the "ugh" feeling. Take note of that feeling in your gut (solar plexus).
2) Inhale: Focus in on the feeling, now inhale (for 7 seconds) the feeling as though you're moving it from your gut to your throat.
3) Exhale: Now expel the feeling from your throat and out of your body, with a sharp exhale for 7 seconds. Hold the breathless state for 3 seconds and feel the emptiness.
4) Repeat this 5 times, until you cannot feel the anxiety/"ugh" feeling in your gut anymore.
5) Now, focus on something you're grateful for. It could be as simple as the pen you're holding. Let the gratitude fill your body up.

Daily Journaling

Recording your thoughts down on pen and paper has a powerful ability to keep you present. The thoughts stop ruminating in your head and reside within the bounds of the journal. For this purpose, I like to journal once after waking (before energy exercises) and once before bed.

The morning journal consists of the first thoughts that come to your head. It does not need to be structured or "perfect"; just a short paragraph to get you started with the day. Here's an excerpt from my journal:

"Monday 1/29/18
  Weekend's over, now back to reality… or can "reality" be a weekend? Perhaps. Tossed and turned all night. Don't wanna get up. Am I afraid of the world? I guess I am a little, but, more excited than afraid. Here's to a great Monday!"

After the free flow writing, proceed to write 3 things that you're grateful for, 3 things that would make the day great and 3 affirmations with "I am …".

The night-time journal entry consists of: 3 amazing things that happened during the course of the day, 3 things that would have made the day better, and a question for the higher self.

Reflecting on the events that occurred during the day gets you more grounded to reality, and eliminates the excuses and beliefs that you use to escape having to do certain things. 3 amazing things makes you more grateful and fuels the affirmations that were made earlier on in the day to make them more prominent in the subconscious; you start to believe that you ARE wealthy, because the amazing thing that happened today was you got $1,000 out of nowhere, reinforcing the "I am wealthy" affirmation.

The question for the higher self can be anything: "How can I make more money", "What am I doing with this engineering degree", "Am I on the right path?" are some of the questions I found myself asking. You either wake up with the answer or receive signs from the world that lead you to the answer. This is also a similar manner in which goals are achieved. The brain has an executive network and a default network; the executive network directs a task i.e. sets the goal, the default network is the creative side that actualizes the goal. When asking a question, or setting a goal, forget about the means to achieve it or the answer you receive, be indifferent to it. The more emotional attachment you have, the more energy potential you generate, and the farther you get from the truth, since nature acts to balance this potential.

3 MANIFESTATION

The All Space

This is a fascinating idea discussed by Vadim Zeland in Transurfing Reality, and even stated in ancient Hermetic Philosophy. Essentially, there exists a space of every single possible outcome, every possible alternate reality. A reality in which you are a wealthy king and live in a palace, and a reality in which you are dirt poor, living on the streets, etc. The All space contains every single possibility, every single outcome. And this space could be contained in your coffee cup, or in outer space, nobody really knows, because we are not capable of conceiving that dimension with our current sensory abilities. Perhaps higher consciousness beings can. We don't need to necessarily have a deep knowledge of this, rather how we can use it to our benefit.

There is nothing to worry about because we are within the All. There is no past, present or future, there merely IS. But presence corresponds most closely the concept of Is-ness, since we are currently incapable of comprehending the higher consciousness. The collection of all possibilities and outcomes is what is called the All, or God; it comes together in One-ness. It's hard to grasp because we are used to thinking about God as one powerful being floating in the air with His legs crossed, or at least I did. What we fail to realize is that since we are made in the image of God, every material, every particle, every thought, thing, energy, comes from God, or the All. We are merely a droplet that has descended from the greater ocean known as the All. That is why we cannot access the same powers as the All is capable of, since we are merely a fraction of it, and also because we THINK that we cannot. This will make sense later.

So the All space can be likened to a film reel that has already been unfolded and laid on the table; to the puny human consciousness, this reel is being unfolded in frames, but to a higher consciousness, all outcomes exist. In order to get an idea of that, imagine your hands moving from left to right; you are seeing it move from left to right, but to a higher consciousness, it already exists in all the positions. Weird isn't it. That is One-ness.

Now you may ask, if all the possibilities already exist, is there any way we can access the reality that we desire? And the answer is YES. At this present moment, you are relaxed and reading this book, but there is a parallel reality in which you are also lounging on top of your penthouse suite in Manhattan, or tasting the delicious food at the finest restaurant in Rome. The sector of the All space that is in existence right now corresponds to the thoughts, self image and what you feel you are worthy of. Every thought resonates at a certain frequency, every feeling amplifies this frequency to manifest that particular sector of the All space. The frequency of the energy that you emanate to the All space corresponds to the quality of your thoughts and beliefs. It may sound disheartening, but you are indeed responsible for the life you are manifesting now. That doesn't mean you cannot manifest the life of your dreams. Armed with this knowledge, you are now capable of shaping your own reality and accessing your desired sector of the All space and bring it into reality. Things will get clearer as you read on.

The Power of Thoughts

> *"Whether you think you can, or you think you can't--you're right."*

-Henry Ford

Every sector of the All space corresponds to a certain frequency. Even your memories that you collect throughout the course of your life do not get stored in your brain, rather it already exists in the All space and has already existed, but the frequency with which you can connect to the memory is stored in your brain. Imagine this scenario: if you had to memorize 10 phone numbers, but you had a phonebook that already has these 10 numbers, in order to access these phone numbers, you merely need to know where the phonebook is kept, why expend energy trying to remember all these numbers? Your brain works in a similar way where it remembers the location in the All space where the memory is stored, by only remembering the frequency with which to connect to it.

Modern science has not been able to prove the All space since it is beyond our comprehension; we are merely trying to take apart a brain to see its contents inside, with disregard for the source it connects to. It's just like if you went back into ancient time with a working TV that utilizes a radio signal for receiving channels, the scientists of that era would take apart the TV to find the content that generates the signal, but the signal is being received via waves through the source, which is beyond the human consciousness to comprehend.

In a similar way, the thoughts that you have emit a certain frequency out into the world, and into the All space. If the frequency of your thoughts matches the frequency of a sector in the All space, then that sector starts materializing. So be very careful what you think, and what you believe in.

This is also why visualization exercises work in manifesting. When you visualize, you tap into the sector of the All space that corresponds to the image that you see. This process is even more vivid in dreams, where we directly access the All space and travel across different sectors of it. But dreams remain just that, dreams. There is no way of materializing dreams since they are accessed in a state of unconsciousness, and without intent.

Apart from corresponding to different sectors in the All space, your thoughts and beliefs also contribute to your self-image, which sets the parameters of what you are capable of attracting into your life. The concept of self-image will be discussed later in this chapter.

Desire vs Intent

We're taught that if we want something badly enough, we will get it. Think about this very carefully. Have you ever wanted something really badly, and you kept wanting it, but things kept going the opposite direction of what you wanted, for example, you wanted to attract a partner, but in desiring and pursuing this attraction, you kept driving him/her away? This happens because desire generates an energy potential, and nature acts to balance the potential by driving away the partner. Now you may ask, why does nature not balance the potential by just attracting the partner to you? Well that's simply because it is much easier for nature to balance the potential by driving the partner away, than by generating attraction in the other person, again nature will always take the path that expends the least energy, in some cases it may just be easier for nature to generate attraction, but most of the time it is not.

So what's a foolproof way of getting what you want? Intent. Intent is the transmutation of desire into action. The energy potential created by desire is transmuted into action, thus it no longer lingers. Think about it this way, you want to get the newspaper, so you place one foot in front of the other, go outside and grab the newspaper. There is very little desire involved. Instead of longing for the newspaper, you merely go out and get it. Next time you long for something, try to apply this attitude. Instead of desiring to have, generate the intent to have and act.

In Transurfing Reality, Vadim Zeland describes intent to consist of inner intention and outer intention. Inner intention is the self-resolve to act against the world in order to get the thing you want. You have transcended desire in longing for something, and are taking active steps towards achieving it. This is very powerful since you are now moving energy via action taking. You aren't getting the thing you want in life yet because energy is not moving through that sector. The morning routine will help you learn how to let energy flow.

Outer intention is when the world gives you the thing that you want, without you having to do anything for it. This is the force that helped the Egyptians build the pyramids or higher consciousness monks use to levitate. You will see opportunities opening up, and you merely have to choose it. There is no need to fight the world. "There is no such thing as a free lunch", this statement is only true if you believe in it. Be careful what you believe in, for you may have to slave away for the rest of your life trying to realize your dreams.

Outer Intention is the most powerful form of intention, yet we cannot control it, thus it's termed "outer". Outer Intention arises once you let go and surrender control on trying to obtain something. So how then can you surrender control but get what you want at the same time? This again goes back to the principle of Balance. You must find your own balance and see what works for you. But in short, it's wanting but being okay with not getting it. Not getting too attached to the outcome, which goes back to Impermanence. Simply trust the universe to do the work for you and allow yourself to have, and you will have tapped into outer intention.

Again, beware of the purposes for which you use this because will generate an energy potential, and nature will act to balance this whether you like it or not. Civilizations that have tapped into the great reserves of Outer Intention, such as the Atlantis, have been wiped out by nature, and now reside underwater. In general, if it is for self-oriented purposes, without causing harm to anyone else, the potential is minimal.

The most powerful method of utilizing the power of Outer Intention, is when you harmonize the connection between the heart and the brain. Contrary to popular belief, the heart actually contains its own brain; an intrinsic nervous system consisting of neurons, neurotransmitters, proteins and support cells. The heart sends far more signals to the brain than the brain does to the heart. The greatest truth resides in your heart; you already have a piece of God in you, but you forget it as you get drawn into the perils of society.

In science, attraction and repulsion is brought about by electromagnetic and electric fields. In humans, this is no different. Once you arise the intent, you attract the things you want in life through the generation of electric and electromagnetic fields. If you have used affirmations for months and months on, and they haven't worked, fret not. The brain is capable of generating both an electric field and an electromagnetic field. But the heart is capable of generating the same fields that are 100 times and 5,000 times greater in strength respectively. Now what do you think is more powerful?

The brain simply thinks, but the heart feels. In order to utilize the heart brain, you must get accustomed to feeling. If you are able to harmonize the connection between the heart and the brain, all the world's blessings will be delivered to you.

Here is an exercise that completely changed my life, it is very primal, and extremely potent:

Harmonizing the heart and brain (10 mins)

1) Sit relaxed and place your palm over your heart with your eyes closed. You don't have to be able to feel the heartbeats; a simple awareness of its position will suffice.
2) Slow down your breathing; 6 seconds on the inhale and 6 seconds on the exhale. Do this for 10 breaths and feel the consciousness shifting from your brain to the place you touch on your body, the heart.
3) This step is crucial. With slowed breathing, feel one or a combination of these emotions: Joy, Care, Gratitude, Compassion. It helps to think about someone or something, and base these emotions off that. Feel these emotions pouring out of your heart and through your

body, and enjoy the feeling of peace that accompanies.
4) Do step 3 for another 10 breaths and open your eyes. Notice how your outlook on life has shifted and enjoy the feeling of relaxation that ensues.

Now you have tapped into the most powerful force in your body. The effects of this exercise will last for more than 6 hours. Aside from massively amplifying the fields that you project into the universe, this exercise also induces self-healing. When you enter such a relaxed state, you essentially tell your body that you are safe, and give permission for the stress hormones to reside and for the healing chemistry to arise. Any injuries, stress or dis-ease (think about this word, it merely means that the body is not at ease due to stress, whether known or unknown to the conscious brain) will slowly heal. You now project high vibration energy at the level of gratitude, love and the like, which all calibrate at the highest level of consciousness and the quality of the things that you will attract from this point forth will correspond to this energy. I like to do this once in the morning and once before bed.

Again, this is just one way in which you can make use of the connection between your heart and mind. There are many other ways, which are even present in everyday life. When making decisions, get accustomed to the way you feel. There will be a resistance when a decision is bad for you, and this is presented by a heavy feeling in the solar plexus. The mind is incapable of knowing as powerfully as the heart; the mind will rationalize and think, but the heart will feel. Again, the harmony between the heart and mind becomes stronger as you learn to become more congruent in what you think and how you feel. If you think a decision is right, make sure it feels right too before making it. Once you get accustomed to getting in touch with your feelings, you slowly tap into the power of Outer Intent, and let the world present things to you.

The 3 Planes of Existence

Consciousness takes on the form of three planes: the spiritual, the mental and the physical. More information on these planes can be found in the Kybalion. The highest and most powerful plane of existence is the spiritual plane. This is connected directly to the All space; everything exists here, angels, demons, God, life, love. All the profound ideas come in this plane and manifest themselves in the mental plane. This is the plane of perceived consciousness. Thoughts reside in the mental plane. For extremely intelligent individuals, this plane is much more vivid, and those with ESP, this plane can be directly bridged with the spiritual plane. Finally, there is the physical plane, which is where we can fully perceive consciousness. Most of human consciousness resides in this plane, thus we are not fully aware of the spiritual and mental planes. We are interested in manifesting our desired reality in the physical plane.

The process of manifestation is as follows: the idea comes to you via a higher power, from the spiritual plane. Higher consciousness individuals are able to access this plane better, and have transcended the mental and physical planes. This is why buddhist monks prefer to retreat into isolation and meditate all the time, for they have experienced the higher states of consciousness, and are unable to function in the linear domain. Typically, these monks have attained the 600+ levels of consciousness, which is the nonlinear domain. David Hawkins briefly talks about the difference between the linear and non-linear domains, but essentially, at the non-linear domain, cause and effect break down and become one; there is no longer a cause and an effect, both bask in the Oneness of life.

The concept of Oneness calibrates as one of the ultimate truths of life. Every particle, every thought, every energy, has emanated from one source, and to the source they shall return. Everything in the existence of the All, has blossomed from the power of the source, the source always was and the source always will be. Once the linear domain is transcended, an individual experiences timelessness, but that doesn't mean that the individual always exists in this state of timelessness.

The idea of the linearity and nonlinearity takes some time, and spiritual awakening to get used to. What is key is the idea that we do not have to live in the linear domain all the time. The most beautiful ideas, creations and emotions are accessed in the non-linear domain. We are accustomed to the $X+Y=Z$; counting one sheep, two sheep, three sheep. No two sheep are alike, but we group them together in one point in space due to simplicity and since our perception cannot grasp any higher. $X+Y$ is not equal to Z, but all X and Y and Z have always been and always will be; to our perception it seems as though the combination of X and Y has caused Z. Of-course you can't just go into work one day and start operating in the non-linear domain, and tell your boss to take a hike. There are times when it's useful to access each of these domains.

As you enter greater and greater spiritual states, everything becomes one. There is perhaps even a phase when you transcend the non-linear realm into complete oneness. If you choose to pursue the path to ultimate spiritual enlightenment, then you are free to do so, but for the purposes of this book, it is sufficient to know when to access the non-linear realm and when to stay in the linear.

The most foolproof way to access the non-linear realm is through feelings and emotions. Emotions do not follow a linear route, and they light up different sectors of the brain and so the All space, which allow you to access mystical qualities that you didn't even know existed. Creative activities allow you to tap into emotions, such as movies, music, painting, and even reading fiction. Once your mind stops operating logically and attunes to feelings, the non-linear domain is accessed. Anything that elicits emotions transfers you to non-linearity.

Now how can one use access to the non-linear realm to manifest great wealth, the partner of their dreams or even an A+ in their next exam? Here's how. Human beings are used to being so linear, and being conditioned to the point where it is frowned upon to feel emotion, that we forget how to get in touch with our emotions in the first place. Emotions are the crucial nuggets in the process of manifesting. He who can control his emotions, can control what he brings into reality from the All space. We are taught that when we get the thing that we want, accomplish our dreams, then we are allowed to feel the emotions. In this case, emotions come AFTER the accomplishment. What you didn't know is that emotions BRING the accomplishment. As discussed previously, emotions are the bridge between all the three planes of existence.

Next time you visualize, imagine you have already accomplished the feat first, and feel the emotions that follow. Open your eyes and bring these emotions to reality. It is one thing to think and see the visual picture of the life of your dreams, it is another thing to FEEL it. Once you start to feel the emotions, you utilize the electric and magnetic fields of the heart, which are again, three and five thousand times greater in power than that of the brain's. Once you visualize, you see the final image, feel the four emotions of: joy, care, gratitude and compassion and relate them to the image. This creates a powerful coherence of the heart and the brain, and makes them resonate at 0.1 hertz, radiating the most powerful magnetic and electric fields, at which both the heart and mind are harmonized to manifest great things.

Self-image

You attract what you are, not what you want. By the age of 12, your subconscious has developed certain beliefs about reality and about the self. However, contrary to popular belief, subconscious beliefs can be altered. Self-image is how you view yourself, and in relevance to the law of attraction, it's the excuses that you make to disallow yourself from experiencing the beauty of life. You may say to yourself "I am tall and handsome" but your subconscious will not register it if, in the past, you have viewed yourself as ugly; it will continue to perceive the self as ugly and unworthy. With this belief, you continue to view yourself through the lens of insecurity, and the quality of things that you attract in your life resonates at that low vibration level of insecurity.

So how then do you change your self-image and let go of all the limiting beliefs in your subconscious? Self-image cannot be changed by intellect or intellectual knowledge, but through experiencing and feeling. This is why people mindlessly use affirmations with no success, because intellectually convincing yourself of your good looks is as futile as wanting and praying for something without taking action to achieve it. Going back to the example of changing the way you perceive yourself, if your affirmation is "I am tall and handsome", instead of mindlessly muttering it, close your eyes and FEEL yourself walking outside into a crowded environment, feeling tall, towering over everyone, exuding confidence. Feel yourself being so handsome that all eyes are on you, and from the sparkle in everyone's eyes you are certain of your attractiveness. Once you utilize feelings, you tap into the powerful magnetic and electric fields of the heart, and reality is manifested much quicker than if you were to mindlessly mutter affirmations. Again, be mindful of your affirmations, since those that are used to bring others down and amplify the ego will generate excess potential, since your will collides with the will of others. Avoid affirmations such as "I am the handsomest in the room", where you compare yourself to others; the only comparison that doesn't generate excess potential is when you compare yourself now to that which you were in the past. Focus on being a better version of you every single day.

Going back to the example of attractiveness, give your affirmations some time, for it takes time to draw in to reality from the All space. The further away your current beliefs are from the self-image you wish to implement, the longer this takes. It is true that sometimes a "face-lift" or braces will dramatically improve your self-image, but that is not because of the action of getting the face-lift or braces; the result of the cosmetic surgery brings about a change in self-image, since it has been ingrained into your subconscious an ideal image that you must assume, thus the surgery brings about a shift in how you perceive yourself. This change in self-perception, from unattractive to attractive, makes you appear more attractive, and attract partners and things that correspond to that vibration. You do not need the cosmetic surgery, merely an emotional and imaginary face-lift.

The concept of self-image is *so* key, since all of your actions and items that you attract correspond to this self-image that you have of yourself. This concept again ties into the principle of Abundance, where life showers you with the things you are already rich in. Even though you do not have money now does not mean you cannot operate from a non-linear domain and assume the outcome; feel and live as though you are wealthy. Live as though a wealthy person would live. Eat and drink like the rich. Wear clothes that the rich would wear. When you visualize, feel what it feels like to have money and the freedom it brings about. It is your birthright to choose your reality. We are all created in the image of "God" or the All, and we all have the ability to shape our own realities just like God creates. No one was placed here on this Earth to slave away at a 9-5 job, work hard to buy the things that you don't want. Always ask yourself what you would rather be doing, always question yourself; awareness is the first step to overcoming a low vibration perception of the self. It has been ingrained into you that you must work a 40 hour week, to make enough money to live and pay rent, and this belief shapes your reality. You are powerful enough to choose your own reality, but you must first realize it. You are in control.

As discussed before, LVE is constantly trying to invade into our lives, and overtake our energy body. We do not have to seek LVE, it finds us, but we must seek HVE and ask it to bless us. Things are happening in our day to day lives that are contributing to the LVE already stored in our subconscious. As you keep practicing the LVE Processing exercise described in the night-time routine, you will see that you feel lighter and lighter every day. This is letting go of the heavy weight of LVE that you are carrying around. Once you start moving out LVE from your energy body, you can flood it with HVE, and this high vibration corresponds to the frequency of things that you will attract into your life. You become more and more malleable, your self-image can easily be shaped and you can implement the new self-image you wish to have of yourself.

Positive self-images can be cultivated and reinforced further into the subconscious through providing proof to the conscious. You can affirm "I am wealthy" or "I am attractive" all you want, but the first proof to the subconscious is the emotions that you feel as you visualize. The last proof is for the conscious mind. As you keep visualizing and feeling the emotions that correspond to the affirmations, you will immediately begin to see results coming in. You will see that girl or guy in your class holding eye contact longer than usual, you will come into an opportunity that will potentially make you a lot of money. In order to really ground the new affirmation, you must perceive any external stimulus that even remotely corresponds to your affirmations to be a RESULT of the affirmation and your visualization. So the belief becomes "she's staring at me, I am therefore attractive". The conscious mind operates in the linear domain, thus the event results in the belief, but the subconscious operates more in the non-linear domain, in which the emotion and the result are synonymous. Once you start grounding the belief in your conscious mind, you are essentially making the affirmation stronger. Now you slowly watch as life unfolds before you, and blesses you in more than you even asked for.

A note of caution. The conscious mind gets very attached to the outcome, it operates at the level of the ego (conscious mind is also the ego-ic mind). Once your self-image is changed, and you consciously start to believe that you are attractive or wealthy, you start expecting that girl you showed interest in to reciprocate or you start expecting that investment to bring in a lot of money. This expecting is good, but the attachment it brings about is not healthy. Attachment and possessiveness violates the principle of Impermanence, thus these feelings generate an energy potential. Nature then acts to balance this potential. Thus the healthy attitude is to appreciate the thing that you have, and show gratitude towards it when you get it. It is yours now, but not forever, enjoy it now that it lasts. No relationship lasts forever, not even marriage, your partner eventually leaves you. No amount of wealth lasts forever, it eventually leaves. Nothing lasts forever. Everything must return to the All. Which brings us to the last step towards manifesting your dreams, letting go of them.

Letting Go

Have you ever desired something for so long, and so badly, that you absolutely needed it and were convinced that you couldn't live without it? You may recall as a child when you wanted a toy or video game very badly, but your parents wouldn't give it to you. You longed for it for a while, but it never came. Eventually, you were preoccupied with other things, and completely forgot about the toy, and as you grew older, you found yourself with better toys, toys that you wouldn't have even dreamt of having when you were younger. But you didn't even notice, until one day it suddenly hit you. "As a child I'd wanted this toy so badly, now I'm playing with even better toys". Perhaps you had a crush on this girl in your class for the longest time. You've wanted to take her out, but it seemed as though your desire was pushing her away. The more you desired her, the more you saw her talking with other boys and the more you pushed her away. Soon, you completely forgot about her, and she just messages you on facebook out of the blue one day, or you even run into her a few years later. You no longer have the intense desire to possess her, for those feelings have been let go. You now easily strike up a friendly conversation with her, and ask her out for dinner, and she agrees. Without any effort, the world delivered to you what you desired for so long. What's going on here?

As discussed before, desire builds up an energy potential, which nature then takes the easiest path to balance out. But, apart from that, desire establishes to the self that you do not already have the thing that you want. When you desire a toy, you establish that you don't already have the toy, thus you enhance the mindset of scarcity, thus life delivers you with more scarcity. Your subconscious now believes that you are worthy of scarcity. Doubts arise, which further enhance the reality of scarcity. Remember that reality depends on your beliefs and the lens through which you wish to view life. If you choose to feel insecure, then life will deliver you events that will amplify this insecurity. If choose to feel confident, then life will deliver you the success that ensues in a confident person's reality. You choose your own reality.

The more and more you desire something, the deeper your desire goes, the more you establish that you don't have the thing that you want, the further you get from what it feels like to own it. You are sucked into the linearity domain, and do not give yourself permission to feel the emotions that you would feel if you had owned it. Remember, feelings are the most important keystones to attracting the desired thing in your life, and the quality of the thing you attract corresponds to the quality of your feelings. If you have lowly feelings of desire, and the victim mindset, then life will deliver you things to amplify this desire. This again goes back to the law of abundance. As you enter gratefulness, life will deliver you things to amplify your gratefulness.

So how do you solve the problem of desire? To intend to have, yes that is powerful. But what also goes alongside intent is to let go of owning something. Realize that you do not need to have it. In the scenarios illustrated above, the key thing that attracted the toy and the girl into reality was letting go. Once you let go of wanting to possess something, you give it the space to attract it. You cannot pursue attract. Attraction is much more powerful than pursuing and chasing. The underlying feelings behind the action of chasing is lust, possessiveness, hate and ego. These all calibrate very low in the consciousness scale. But attraction has feelings of love, appreciation and gratefulness. When you chase something and you get it, you become insecure of losing it. When you attract something and you get it, you learn to appreciate it.

Letting go allows the world to do the work in order to get it, and when you chase and desire something, you expend energy and resist the world in order to get it. See the difference? This is not to say that you must not take action to manifest the life of your dreams. Realize the place and the FEELINGS the action taking is coming from. If you are taking action from the place of scarcity and lack, then you will never get it. If you are taking action from abundance, then every step of the action you take will feel right. The difference between doing something from abundance and doing something from scarcity is the feeling of want versus need. When you NEED something, you act from scarcity. When you do something simply because you want to, then you act from abundance. Think of a man who has very little financial means, and he decides to work to support himself and his family. Now think of a man who has a million dollars but decides to become a school teacher, simply because he enjoys teaching. In the former case, the man works because he is in need; he operates out of scarcity and this job is a means for him to survive. In the latter case, the man works simply because he enjoys teaching; the underlying feelings behind the action of teaching are those that emanate an abundance mindset. Realize that in every task in life that you do, you do not NEED to do anything. Once you can let go of need, and operate out of abundance then you attract more abundance into your life. Like attracts like.

You may ask: "How can I want something yet let go of wanting it?". This is indeed the ultimate paradox of life. As mentioned in the principle of Balance, nature acts to balance everything out, all energy potentials that are generated are eventually brought to nought. Letting go of the desire to achieve something is your way of keeping the energy potential to a minimum, so nature doesn't have to take it away from you. Having the intent to have creates no potential since there is no thought involved; you do not desire to raise your arm, you simply raise it. The more you practice letting go of your grip of control, the better you get at mastering your intent.

There are two beliefs that help you want something yet

let go of achieving it. The first is an understanding of the principle of Impermanence. Knowing that everything in life is temporary, as you achieve events in life, come from a mindset of "If I get it, that's amazing, if I don't, my life is already amazing". All is fleeting anyways. You also realize that you are complete already. You do not NEED anything, you simply want it because you would like to appreciate it for the temporary period that you may have it in your possession. This is why operating from gratefulness and appreciation brings about the best things in life.

The last, and most powerful belief to have is the realization that life is your friend, and everything is going as it should. When you start to believe that life is truly your friend, then life only delivers beautiful things to you. Everything starts to radiate love. The trees, the buildings, the grass and the streets. You start to radiate love outwards. You completely let go in the belief that nature will deliver to you better things that you even ask for. Recall the discussion of the idea of a subjective reality and the lens that shapes your reality. If you start to view life through the lens of "life is my best friend, everything is unfolding as it should", what do you think will happen? Life will shower you with all its blessings. You merely ask life for something and let go of the control and means to achieve it, and life presents you with the opportunities or even delivers them to your front door. Such is the power of this belief. If you can adopt a powerful belief and ingrain it into your being, then you do not even need any other technique in this book. This alone will suffice.

☐

4 WHEN THINGS AREN'T GOING YOUR WAY

Negative Thoughts and their Harmfulness

As children, whenever we wouldn't receive a toy, we'd merely throw a tantrum and our parents would bring us the toy. We grow up to find comfort in throwing tantrums whenever we don't get the thing that we desire. As an adult, whenever life isn't going our way, we sometimes fall into this temporary "depression". It gets more and more difficult to wake up each morning, new projects started with an attitude of enthusiasm eventually dies out to apathy. "What's the point?" we find ourselves asking. It's almost as though you're waiting for something good to happen.

This feeling is more prominent once you've had a streak of good fortune, or a period of time when your needs were met and you were in high spirits because of some external events that went your way. This is a classic sign of attachment. The principle of Impermanence indicates that nothing is forever. Life will present itself in highs and lows; there will always be a period of highs and a period of lows. If you are riding the high waves, expect to ride the low waves. Once you start deriving the source of your energy from external events, you become attached to the highs and lows of life.

It is very easy to fall into the victim mindset, where you feel as though the world owes you something. You look at those who are wealthier, better looking or someone that appears to have it much easier than you do, and you feel envy. "Why couldn't I be born with those looks", "If I had that kind of money I would …". But the truth is, everyone has problems. The wealthy man may probably be struggling with chronic stress or even problems in the family. What appears at the surface doesn't necessarily represent what's beneath. We all have problems, it's how you deal with it that counts.

Remember, any negative thought is like a disease to your body, and to your spirit. The more negative thoughts you focus on, the more of negativity you attract into your life. Such is the law of abundance. If you are abundant in negative thoughts, then life will provide you with more negative events. We are always focused on what we want to avoid, as opposed to what we want to achieve. Recall that outer intent manifests whatever the heart and mind comes together in. If you are thinking about the flu that's going around, and you feel fear in your heart of catching it, then you are bringing together the mind and the heart in the emotion of fear and thoughts of the flu, then the power of outer intent will bring about the flu into your life. Thus it is always the case that whatever we fear, we manifest it with very little effort on our part, whereas it seems vastly difficult to manifest the good things that we want. This again, is because the emotion of your fear you feel with much more power than the love or gratefulness. The more love you feel, and the more you focus on what you do want, the powerful the fields you radiate in attracting your dreams into reality.

LIFE MASTERY

The 4 Step Process to Eliminate Negative Thoughts

Here's an easy exercise I've used as soon as I start to have negative thoughts. This method came to me after years and years of trying to avoid the obvious, resisting the negative thoughts, and I'd finally figured out that running into the fog is better than running away from the fog that keeps chasing you, the only escape is to the other side. Once you learn to eliminate negative thoughts from your life, you are left with positive thoughts, and the quality of the things you attract correspond to the vibration of positivity. Eliminating negativity is the first step to entering high vibration energy. Recall how we moved out LVE out of our body to make room for HVE in the morning routine. The following exercise is on the go, it can be done very quickly and dynamically, for when LVE catches a grasp on you.

<u>Exercise to Eliminate Negativity (5-10 mins)</u>

1) <u>Awareness:</u> As you did in the morning routine, close your eyes for a few seconds and go into your body. Identify any knots or tenseness. The heavy feeling that resides in your solar plexus is most common for all. This is your body's way of saying that something is not right. The first step is the most crucial step; you cannot get rid of something that you cannot even identify.
2) <u>Acknowledgment</u>: Now that you've identified the tense and heavy feeling and where it presents itself, accept it. The less you try to resist this feeling, the less it will feed off the energy of your resistance. Feel this tenseness, amplify this tenseness even more. Now try to spin this feeling, see if it can move clockwise or counterclockwise; into the plane of the body and out. Now you are gaining control of it. This technique is a very powerful Neuro Linguistic Programming (NLP) technique.
3) <u>Let go</u>: You are now in control of the feeling. Keep

going deeper into it and take three deep breaths. This is similar to the letting go exercise of the night routine. Breathe into the negative feeling and exhale it out of your body. Upon your last exhale, imagine the feeling moving out of your body and dissipating into the mist.
4) <u>Reframe</u>: Evil can only be overcome with goodness. As you feel the negative thoughts dissipating, now is the time to replace them with one thing that you feel love and gratitude for. It could be a smiling picture of your mother, and you hug her, or any other thing that fills you up with the warm, loving feeling in your heart.

Congratulations, you have now eliminated negativity and bask in love. As you keep doing this exercise, you get quicker and better at identifying your own emotions. I like to go about the day and just go into my body to see how I'm feeling to see if there is any tenseness. On the path to your dreams, you cannot even afford a single drop of negativity or negative thoughts into your life. As you enter into greater states of HVE, you'll notice that your previous LVE habits no longer energize you, rather they suck your energy away. You slowly begin to eat healthier, without even noticing. You begin to surround yourself with people who also radiate positivity; participating in gossip no longer pleases you. You attract more positivity in your life.

Negativity = Positivity in Disguise

While the eradication of negative thoughts from one's life is crucial, negativity can also be used to fuel the law of attraction working in your favor. Remember how we said that your beliefs act as a lens through which you view reality? Well, if you start to reframe negativity into positivity, then even the negative events that occur in your life will allow the universe to manifest your dreams in your favor.

The key belief that allows you to adopt a lens that turns negativity into positivity was discussed above. It is: "everything is unfolding as it should, this was meant to happen". Think about all the "bad" things that happened in your life. Your break-up with your beloved partner, losing your job, failing an exam, losing a lot of money. Now ask yourself if these events occurred all at the perfect time. Funny isn't it? Life has a way of knowing what needs to happen when. It is beyond our power to understand why life does the things that it does. Essentially, all these negative circumstances HAD to occur to allow you to be here in the place you are now. Now ask yourself this. If life had to get you fired from a job that you absolutely despise, pays little and all your co-workers treat you terribly, in order to make way for the dream job, that pays you more money than you care about, would you be so upset? Don't be so quick to judge all the events in life. Perceived bad things must happen in order to make way for better things to come. Once circumstances that are perceived as "negative" occur in your life, it means that you are shifting to a lifeline of your visions; life is going as it should, everything is unfolding according to plan. Just keep placing one foot in front of the other, and have the image of your final destination in mind. For me, this is a mansion in the cliffs, surrounded by mesmerizingly blue waters. I'm standing with the woman of my dreams, watching as the waves crash at the bottom of the cliff, and the sun setting in the distance only to whisper into her ear "baby we made it". Do not worry too much about the means by which you have to achieve your goal yet, it will come to you. Just keep picturing the final destination.

Now you are armed with the powerful tool of the reframe; turning perceived negative events into positive events. Once you start believing that you will shape your reality with your beliefs.

Using Negativity as a Fuel for Presence

The present moment is the moment that really is. This is the ultimate truth. Once you become more present to the moment, you start to tap into the heavenly powers that energize your thoughts into reality. Little did you know that you could use the negative thoughts and events in your life to drive you deeper into Presence.

Consider this scenario. You just stubbed your toe, and you feel a sharp pain going up your leg, concentrated on the toe. You cannot think, or feel anything else but the pain. You no longer think about what to do afterwards, or what happened yesterday, you are completely focused on the pain because it is overriding everything else. This pain is making you more present. You draw on this present energy until it heals the pain of the stubbed toe. Presence has powerful healing properties. I'm not saying you must inflict pain upon yourself to draw on the power of Presence, rather providing an instance that gives you no choice but to be present. A good practice for getting present is to exercise or take a cold shower. Practice taking a cold shower every morning for 21 days. Feel the icy cool water drops strike your skin, and feel into the cold. It's difficult, but it makes you intensely present. The more pain you feel, the more in touch with your feelings you get and the more present energy you draw into your life. I cannot explain to you the full extent of the magical properties of the present moment, but life rewards you the more you accept its Truth; see for yourself as you practice getting more present throughout the day.

All the negative events that occur into your life is nature's way of making you more present. Nature doesn't see any event as positive or negative, it just gives strives to balance the energy potential created, and expends the least amount of energy to achieve the balance. Presence is your key to balancing the energy potential yourself, and taking on the reigns to control your life. Always remember that you were meant to choose your own reality; manifesting the life of your dreams should never be a struggle, it all feels right and falls into place like the pieces of a puzzle. If you feel resistance, then the goals and dreams you set are not the ones that your heart wants, rather they have been conditioned to you by society and LVE sources that seeks to take your energy away. Remember, there can never be a problem in the present moment.

Now you know that you cannot afford even a single droplet of negative thoughts. Imagine the greatness you would manifest if you were only filled with positivity. The final method of getting deeper into presence is to tap into the emotion of gratitude. The feeling of gratitude generates a powerful healing sphere around you. You start to radiate love. Once you feel grateful, you start to appreciate the things, the people and the life you already live. You start to tap into Oneness and divinity, and the self starts to realize that it is already complete. You realize that you do not need anything. You may ask, "well if I feel complete, then why would I need the partner, the money and the life of my dreams?". To that, the answer is yes. Simply that you do not NEED anything, you want it because you want to appreciate it, for everything is ephemeral. You feel grateful of what you already have, the things that you once had and appreciated for a while, the things you currently have, and the things that you will have. All is encapsuled in the divine feeling of gratitude. When you visualize and see yourself in the yacht that you own, or the business deal that you are successfully closing, or standing atop a hill with the partner of your dreams, it makes you feel grateful. Tap into that feeling of gratitude and start to link that feeling with the things you currently own. For example, the bed you're lying down on, feel grateful for it, the same gratitude you feel once you're with your beloved in your visions, and you will start to radiate energy at the frequency that attracts that reality into reality from the All space.

The beauty of the feeling of gratitude is that it instantly dissolves negativity. As you reframe your negative thoughts into positive thoughts, reframing with gratitude becomes a powerful reminder to your body to stop focusing on the negatives and start focusing on the positives. As you already know, you attract the things your thoughts are focused on.

5 LIFE AS A DREAM

Dear reader, you now have all the tools and techniques required to shape your reality. Remember that this life is nothing but a dream, the higher you reach in your states of consciousness, the more you detach from this dream and start to realize your higher self. When performing the practices outlined in this book, please reserve judgment for 21 days; this is the time it takes for a habit to form and for the effectiveness of any practice to show. You will see that you will develop a new best friend: life. Life will start to bless you in gifts that you haven't even asked for, it will deliver you with better gifts than you visualized.

From time to time, we all get exhausted by the repetitiveness of our daily lives, and often it seems like nothing is going to plan. Just keep faith, and please do not get attached to the wave of life; every good period is followed by its counter. The only way you can ensure this attachment does not occur is to become present, and feel gratitude every day for everything that is now. As you manifest the life of your dreams, remember that you are not wishing for it; you merely have the intent and you manifest the sector of the All space that corresponds to your intent. You may wish and desire all you want, but in doing so you are distancing yourself further from your dreams through the generation of an energy potential. Everyone has the right to choose the life they want, we were not put into this world to slave away at desk jobs to earn enough money for the things that we do not even want. It is true that you need to work hard, but there should never be a resistance to it, and even working hard for the right goal should feel enjoyable, thus you enjoy every step of the process.

Finally, remember to enjoy the gifts life gives you, for the feeling of gratitude corresponds to unconditional love; this is the highest attainable state of consciousness in the linear domain. Not only will gratitude start the chain of events that bring good fortune into your life, but it will allow you to wake up from the daydream of life and seize your reality. Just as in your dreams you get to control them if you realize that you are dreaming, in waking this also corresponds to increasing your state of consciousness. Practicing lucid dreaming will not necessarily ensure that you become more "awake" in reality; dreams are non-transferrable to the waking state. The only way to become more awake is to become more present, that is why the principle of Presence has been emphasized throughout this book. Good luck and take care

ABOUT THE AUTHOR

Quazi Johir is currently an undergraduate, studying mechanical engineering at Boston University. Having lived in five different continents by the age of 18, he was always curious about the changing nature of the world. Until 2017 he sought answers, but after a spiritual awakening, he found that the answer does not matter, but the question asked. He currently runs a Youtube channel under his name, *Quazi Johir,* where he shares his experiences in implementing various advice from spiritual authorities, books and even his own findings, as he has done so in this book, his first, *Life Mastery.*

Made in the USA
Las Vegas, NV
06 April 2024